Acknowledgements

I would like to thank people who have inspired me in the past: my mother who encouraged me onto this path.

My friends and colleagues, especially Violet A. Cordy, Rani M. Johnson, Doctor Helena Ovens, and clients with whom over the years have supported me in my quest. My partner Jan K who has given me the space and support for me to write this book.

To Coco The Aroma Shoppe Dog

Table of Contents

Preface to the first edition

CHAPTER ONE

Pet Care 3

Essential Oils 4

    Using Essential oils on Cats, Dogs and Horses 5

Essential Oils: A brief history 9

What are Essential Oils? 10

How to use essential oils 13

Cautions 16

The Most Useful Essential Oils in Pet Care 19

Vegetable Oils & Extracts 33

CHAPTER TWO

Why make your own pet care products? 41

Tools of the Trade 42

Cautions when making products: 43
Shampoo 44
    Experimental Basic Shampoo 44
    Shampoo Base 46
    Doggie Shampoo 47
    Sparkle and Shine Shampoo 48
    Chamomile Shampoo 48
Conditioners 49
    Experimental Basic Conditioner 49
    Jojoba Conditioner 50
    Conditioning Oil 52

CHAPTER THREE

Common disorders 53
    Arthritis and Rheumatism (aches and pains) 53
    Eczema 55

    Psoriasis 56

RECIPES and TREATMENTS 57

    Healing Ointment 57

    Eczema oil 59

    Anti-stress 59

    Aches and Pains 60

    Arthritis and Rheumatism 60

    Bad Odour Spray 61

    Fur tonic 62

    Bug Spray 63

    Hot Spot Itch relief Spray 64

CHAPTER FOUR

Designing a Blend 65

    Aromatic Blending 69

    The Art of Blending 73

Tables..79

    The Basics...79

    Proper Measurement..80

Therapeutic Cross Reference Chart..81

    Digestive Disorders..82

    Head and Neck Disorders..84

    Muscular and Joint Disorders..85

    Fur and Skin Disorders..87

    Mental/Emotional Symptoms..90

    Misc. Disorders..96

CHAPTER FIVE

Starting Your Pet Care Business...97

    Ingredients needed before making the products presented in this book..........................101

    Final Word..103

About the Author..108

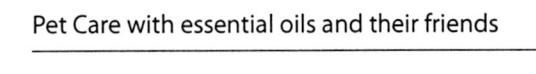

Pet Care with essential oils and their friends

Preface to the first edition

Welcome to the first edition of Pet Care with essential oils and their friends.

This book, although using the elements and accumulated knowledge of aromatherapy, is focused on natural products for pets and on the making of products. Essential oils play an important role in holistic health care for pets, consequently, I have included information about essential oils that are the most useful in pet care, *as well as the essential oils to avoid!*

As a cosmetic maker, and holistic practitioner since 1978, I have been appalled at the lack of 'unclean' pet products available on the market, and the use of 'unsafe' essential oils such as tea tree that is often one of the ingredients that are in holistic pet shampoos.

Over the years I have developed and produced shampoos, conditioners and treatments for horses, dogs and cats. The recipes are straight forward and easy to follow, and, as long as you are patient, the results will be rewarding.

In the treatment recipe section, I have included some recipes that I have used on my pets and client's pets over the years. Do not limit yourselves to the ingredients listed; there is much more to be discovered. Experiment, be creative and above all have fun.

Jan Benham

CHAPTER ONE

Pet Care

Western veterinary physicians, except for a few enlightened exceptions, still regard our pets like a car and discuss problems and solutions in mechanical terms. If the body is not working properly, for example, the solution is to find and change the defective part or in some way modify it. In reaction to this mechanistic medicine, there has been a phenomenal growth in holistic alternatives.

How do the above limitations of Western veterinary practices relate to natural pet care? The pharmaceutical and big business pet care companies try to synthesize and duplicate what already occurs in nature. The sticky debate is that in a living organism there is something more than the sum of its component parts. Whether we are discussing a human being, animal or a naturally occurring plant product, there is always a "life force" energy that is present. The scientific community resists any attempt to link itself with this sort of mysticism and unfortunately rejects most holistic approaches in health care for pets.

How did the pet care industry become so alienated from nature? It got seduced by the easy availability of petroleum by-products and their ability to be patented. Not only are these by-products less effective in treatments for skin conditions such as eczema and dermatitis, we then add the harmful effects of synthetic dyes and preservatives such as formaldehyde, and parabens to the mix. *For more information, see the chapter on politically incorrect ingredients for natural cosmetics in the Creamy Craft of Cosmetic Making Book.*

In contrast to commercial ready-made cosmetics, the homemade ones offered in these pages make exclusive use of natural substances. They contain no mineral oils, animal products in any form i.e. lanolin or gelatin, synthetic substances, synthetic preservatives or dyes.

Essential Oils

Smell is an important primeval sense. The first major nerve that enters the brain detects aroma. That nerve - and information it carries connects directly to the base of the brain where immediate responses occur. Emotions are highly influenced by aromas, good aromas calm and attract while bad aromas repel and cause aggravation. Our pets use their sense of smell to gain all sorts of complex information from the environment and this information is used to calculate and predict what states of energy and response they should adopt.

The use of essential oils has been found to be helpful for both emotional and physical health in both animal and human care. We are becoming more aware of ways we can use our pets noses to assist their health and emotional well-being. If you start using essential oils on "Chucky", it is important that you learn a bit about the subject. And, since animals and humans are different, it is important to know how to properly use oils in pets so that we do not unwittingly harm them in the process.

Using Essential oils on Cats, Dogs and Horses

As a pet owner and a holistic health practitioner for most of my life I have always used essential oils and natural products on my dogs, cats and horses.

Animals vary so much in their sensitivity to essential oils. Tier, my malamute dog didn't like the smell of most essential oils, whereas Coco (Jack Russell and Chihuahua mix) just loved them and was around every time I was decanting or making up a blend. She became known as the Aroma Shoppe dog!

It is interesting to note that in the wild, animals pick and choose the healing plants they need to help them stay in optimal health; it is possible that your animal using its own instinct through a sniff test can choose which essential oils would be of most help to them. I have used this method time and again and found it effective.

The basic principles of using essential oils on animals are the same whatever the species, although there are differences in dilutions.

For example with **horses** you can allow your horse to lick a small amount of diluted essential oil/s (this can be a blend of different essential oils or just one) from your hand, anywhere from 1 drop to a maximum of 10 drops of essential oil mixed in carrier oil per session. Often horses just want to smell the essential oil, especially if it is an emotional problem. If your horse does not want the essential oil he will turn his head or move away from you and it's important to give him the space to do this.

If he seems to like the essential oil, offer your horse the essential oil blended in carrier oil once or twice a day until he loses interest, usually within three to nine days. Sometimes horses will show interest in one essential oil for one session then show no interest. Once your horse shows no further interest in the essential oils, they are no longer needed and you should have seen improvement in the condition.

On the other hand with **cats**, hold the closed bottle of essential oils at least 6 inches away from your cat's nose. Be patient and allow the cat to come towards the bottle if it wants to, rather than going towards the cat. Once you are sure the cat likes the oil (see responses below), dilute one drop into 10ml of cold-pressed vegetable oil.

- Signs of a keen interest: Smelling intently, licking the lips or trying to lick the bottle, follows you around with the aroma, rolls on its back, rubs against you – offer diluted oil once or twice daily.
- Signs of a moderate interest: A few sniffs then walks away, a small sniff but returns to the bottle, tongue licks quickly, easily distracted from the aromas – offer diluted oil once a day.
- No Interest: Turns away from the aroma, leaves the room – Do not apply.

With **dogs**, use the same method as with horses except use less essential oil, anywhere from 1 drop to 6 drops per session. Always start off with small amounts and work up!

Caution: Essential oils are invaluable for use in dog care especially for "doggie" smells, skin conditions, arthritis, bug repellents and in healing salves etc. However, certain essential oils such as Tea Tree could possibly be toxic to dogs and cats but unfortunately can be found in everything from pet shampoo to flea treatments.

Pet Care with essential oils and their friends

Essential Oils: A brief history

Since our records from Atlantis are still a little vague, Egypt figures as the beginning of our "essential" story. Essential oils in ancient Egypt were used in healing, in temple rituals, for perfumes and embalming. At about the same time, the Indians and Chinese were also developing the use of plant materials in healing.

In the Middle Ages, essential oils and herbs were often used on the skin to mask the unhygienic conditions of the era, and as the use of herbs and essential oils became more widespread and what was useful became more apparent.

Modern essential oil usage dates to Rene Maurice Gattafosse a French chemist around the turn of the century who discovered the healing properties of lavender oil after burning his hand in a laboratory accident which led to a life - long research on essential oils and their properties. "Aromatherapie: Les huiles essentielles hormones vegetales", the first book on aromatherapy, was published by Gattefosse in 1937.

During the Second World War, another pioneer Doctor Jean Valnet used oils in the treatment of wounded soldiers and subsequently developed the use of essential oils for internal use, now practiced by medical doctors in France. Dr. Valnet wrote the book "The Practice of Aromatherapy". Modern day phyto aromatherapy is the grandchild of Dr. Valnet's studies.

Madame Maury, the mother of modern aromatherapy developed the field of the use of essential oils via massage and smell. She was the inspiration for Shirley Price, Daniele Ryman and other pioneers in aromatherapy. Madame Maury's "Guide to Aromatherapy", was first published in the French language in 1961.

Unfortunately very little has been documented on the use of essential oils in pet care. I suspect that enlightened people in the Middle Ages who used herbal remedies for themselves, also used them for their pets as well.

The use of essential oil therapy as a healing art in itself has been a very recent phenomenon. For more reading about natural pet care, herbal books such as Culpepper's *The Complete Herbal* (1653) contains valuable information about the use of herbs in pet care.

What are Essential Oils?

Essential oils are odorous and highly volatile (they readily evaporate in the open air). They are extracted by various methods, usually by steam distillation from plants, herbs, flowers, seeds, grasses, roots, trees and fruits.

Essential oils are not to be confused with "fragrance oils" which have no therapeutic effect upon the body like pure essential oils do.

Essential oils used in natural pet care are the results of collective knowledge gained over thousands of years from many contributing countries. With that being said, aromatherapy for pets is a bit more complicated than it is for humans!

Essential oils have marvellous therapeutic properties, and together with their medicinal capabilities, are known and recognized all over the world. All essential oils are anti-bacterial, and many of them are anti-viral and anti-fungal.

They are natural and achieve the desired results that cannot be gained through the use of synthetics because essential oils can be classed as **biotic (Strengthens living tissue whilst destroying bacteria), which is the opposite of anti-biotic.**

Essential oil therapy, also known as *Aromatherapy*, works directly on the skin and organs, and has a direct effect on the limbic system in the brain. Essential oils work on many levels, externally applied they penetrate the skin and reach the blood stream in minute quantities to heal muscles and organs, whilst at the same time there is an immediate effect upon our emotions through the smell penetrating our noses. Essential oils can help with a physical condition whilst reducing anxiety at the same time.

Pet Care with essential oils and their friends

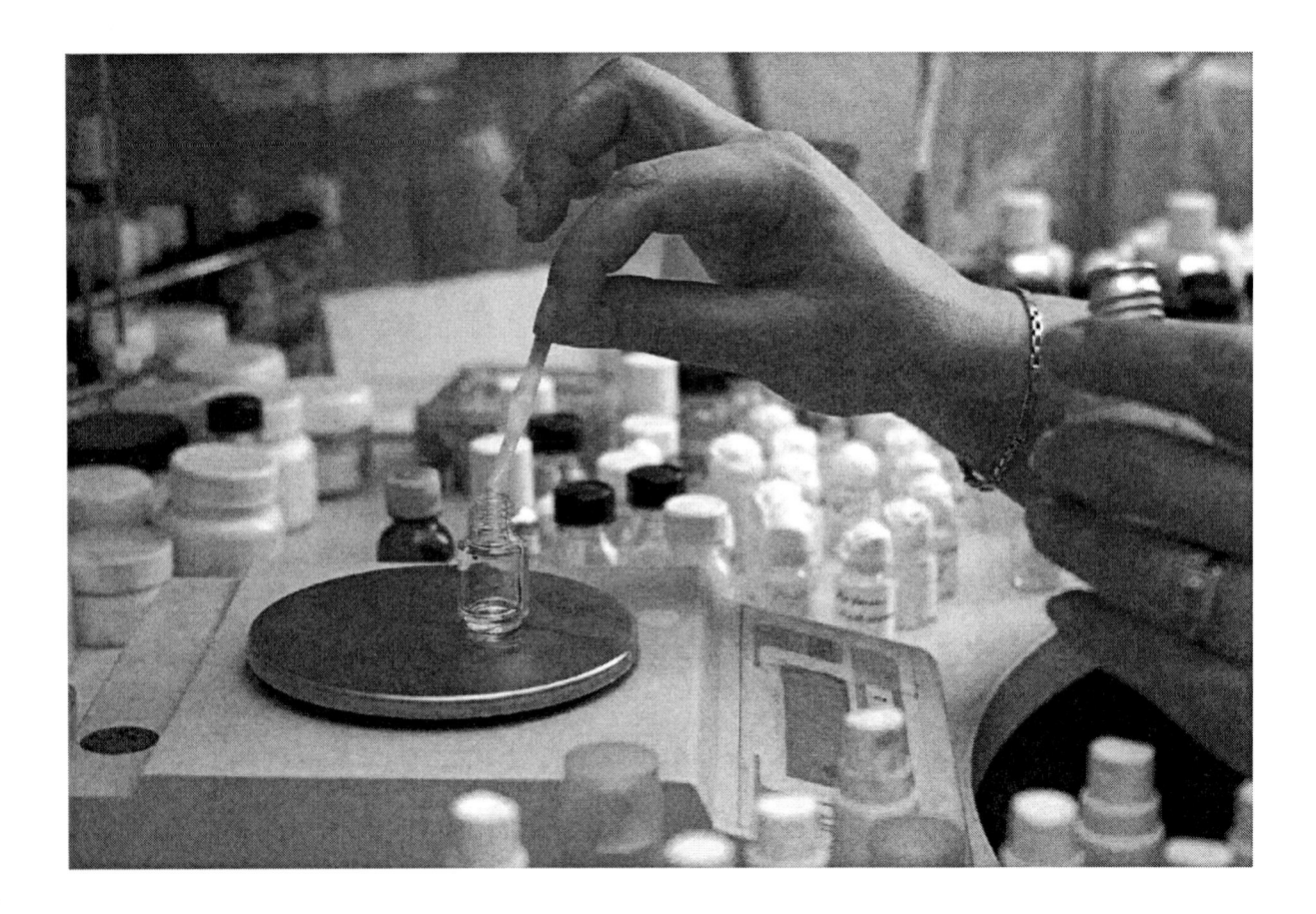

How to use essential oils.

Essential oils are very concentrated and should be used with care. Apart from a few exceptions, they should NOT BE USED directly on the skin but dissolved in vegetable oil, alcohol or water.

Internally (ingested)

Essential oils can be administered to horses via a capsule and mixed with the feed. A few drops (1 to 3) could be added to gravy on food when administering to dogs. Do NOT administer essential oils to cats internally.

WARNING: Essential oils should **not** be given to animals internally without extensive essential oil knowledge or consultation with a holistic vet!

Inhalation

Add up to 3 drops on a tissue and let your pet breathe in, if it is not good for "Chucky" then he/she will let you know!

Massage or application

Add 1 drop to 5 ml of carrier oil see 'using essential oils on cats, dogs and horses' and 'designing a blend' (pages 5 and 65).

For a carrier oil, it is best to use pure, fine and cold pressed vegetable oils such as sweet almond oil, Sunflower, Olive and Calendula.

Areas to apply essential oils on your pets:

For non-ungulate animals (not having hooves) such as dogs and cats, oils can be applied to the paws for faster absorption.

For hoofed animals, good places to apply mixed oils would be on their spine or flanks and massaged in. Also on the frog and cornet bands of hooves. Oils can also be applied to the auricular points of the ears.

For applying to a large wound or hard to reach areas, it helps to put the essential oils in a spray bottle diluted with a carrier oil.

Horses can have the highest concentration of essential oils i.e. starting at 3 drops of essential oil to a 10 drops maximum mixed in carrier oil, per application.

(1% to 5%)

Dogs: From 1 drop to a maximum of 6 drops mixed in carrier oil per application, this depending on the breed and size of the dog!

(1/2 % to 3%)

Cats: You are looking at very high dilutions of essential oils, 1 drop to 10mls of carrier oil, (as little as 1 drop to 25mls can be effective).

(1/8th to 1/2 %)

Compresses These can be hot /or cold.

Add 3 to 10 drops of essential oils to a bowl of water. Soak a cloth in the blend of essential oils and water, wring the cloth and then apply to the affected area.

Sprays

Fill a plant sprayer with water and add a few drops of essential oil/s. Shake vigorously before use. Oils can be diluted in a little vodka/witch hazel before adding water.

Neat application

Apply 1 drop undiluted onto blemishes, cuts and burns (Lavender), and for the relief of insect bites and stings (Geranium). Caution: Never use essential oils neat on cats!

Cautions:

- Animals have an extremely good sense of smell, so in most cases it is best to use oils that are diluted and to always provide an escape route. If a pet does not like an essential oil, do not enforce its use. Use oils sparingly on cats as they are particularly at risk for oil reactions.

- Use 100% pure, therapeutic grade essential oils on your pets (and humans).

- Use only essential oils that are safe for your pet. Essential oils such as cinnamon, clove, oregano, wintergreen, thyme, tea tree, birch, and any other oils containing phenols should never be used on cats and with caution on dogs and horses, as these oils can cause liver and kidney toxicity.

- Essential oils should not be used undiluted on the skin except under guidance of a holistic vet.

- Dilute essential oils before using them. A rough guideline is to add about 1 - 15 drops of essential oils to 15ml of carrier oil. Sometimes essential oils are used neat in certain situations.

- Use less amount of diluted oils on puppies, senior animals and those whose health is compromised. When in doubt start off with hydrolates (floral waters).
- Do not administer essential oils internally unless under the guidance of a holistic vet.
- Check with a holistic vet before using any essential oils on pregnant pets. In particular, do not use stimulating oils (e.g. peppermint, rosemary, eucalyptus, tea tree, niaouli) on pregnant dogs, horses or cats.
- Keep essential oils away from children and pets.
- Essential oils in or close to the eyes, directly on or close to the nose, or in the anal or genital areas is a big **no-no.**
- Check for contra indications.
- Don't use oils on epileptic dogs or dogs who are seizure-prone. Some oils such as rosemary, may trigger seizures (in humans too).
- Essential oils are flammable, so do not put them on or near a naked flame.
- Essential oils may damage certain plastics and polished wood surfaces.

Pet Care with essential oils and their friends

Citrus bergamia

18

The Most Useful Essential Oils in Pet Care

BERGAMOT *(Citrus bergamia)*

Bergamot because of its antifungal and soothing properties, makes a good choice for treating inflammatory skin disorders such as eczema and dermatitis. Bergamot is excellent for ear infections caused by yeast or bacterial overgrowth.

A hot compress of bergamot and eucalyptus can be used on boils to draw out the infection. Do not use bergamot undiluted as it can cause skin irritation.

CARROT SEED *(Daucus carota)*

This essential oil, not to be confused with carrot root oil, promotes healthy skin, coat and hooves in horses and dogs and is anti-inflammatory. Good for psoriasis and eczema, dry, flaky and sensitive skin. Can rejuvenate and stimulate tissue regeneration, thus effective for scar healing. Helpful to use if an animal has been physically or emotionally abandoned.

Chamaemelum nobile

CHAMOMILE
ROMAN CHAMOMILE *(Anthemis nobilis)*

Chamomile is antiseptic, antispasmodic, and good for soothing the central nervous system. Effective for relief of muscle pains, cramps and teething pain. For the skin, it helps relieve sensitive, dry and itchy skin, Chamomile is non-toxic, gentle and safe to use.

A "must-have" for dogs and horses!

CEDARWOOD *(Juniperus virginiana)*

Cedarwood was valued highly by the ancient Egyptians and was used in the embalming and mummification process. Cedarwood is antiseptic, tonifying, stimulates the circulation. Good for skin and coat conditioning, eczema, psoriasis and dermatitis of all types. Flea-repelling.

Note: In high concentrations it will irritate the skin.

CLARY SAGE *(Salvia sclarea)*

Clary sage is nerve-calming, gentle when used in small amounts and properly diluted. Sedates the central nervous system. On an emotional level, clary sage is great for leaving the past behind and moving forward.

Pet Care with essential oils and their friends

Boswellia carterii

EUCALYPTUS *(Eucalyptus radiata)*

Eucalyptus is anti-viral, anti-inflammatory, an expectorant. Helps relieve chest congestion and effective in repelling fleas. Note: Eucalyptus radiata is gentler to use than eucalyptus globulus, which is the most common type of eucalyptus used.

FRANKINCENSE *(Boswellia carteri)*

Frankincense has an astringent, rejuvenating and beneficial effect upon the skin, healing to wounds and excellent for inflammation. In fact it has been suggested that it might be helpful for both skin and other types of cancer. On an emotional level, frankincense helps with stress, anxiety and depression, it reminds us to breathe! Helps with unworthiness and insecurity.

HELICHRYSM *(Helichrysm italicum)*

Helichrysm, also known as everlasting and immortelle, is anti-inflammatory, analgesic and has incredible regenerative effects for skin conditions and irritations (e.g. eczema). Effective for the healing of scars and bruises, and for pain relief. Helps with bruised emotions and cuts through emotional blocks in a gentle way.

Pet Care with essential oils and their friends

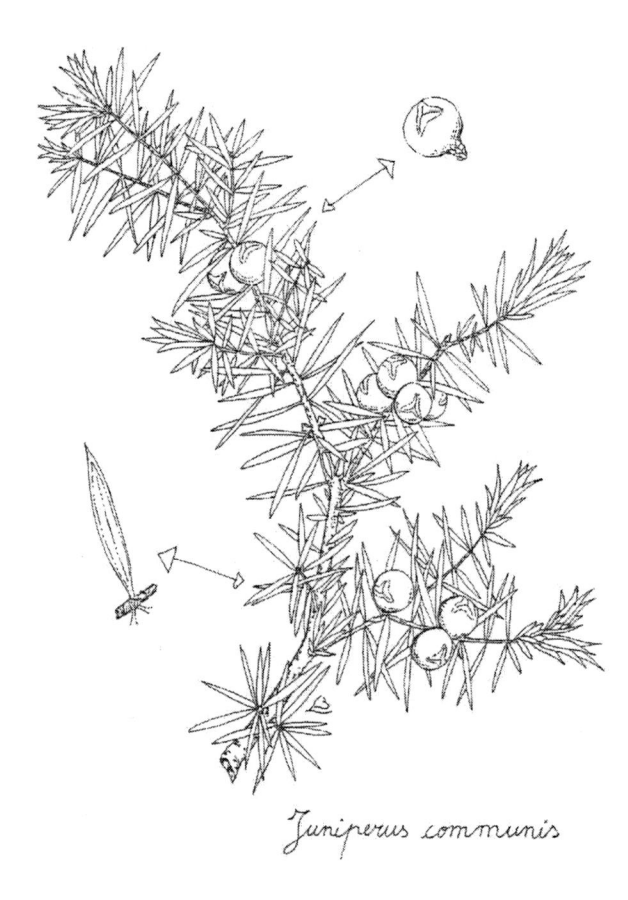

Juniperus communis

GERANIUM *(Pelargonium graveolens)*

Geranium has a cleansing, refreshing and astringent effect on the skin and helps relieve inflamed and irritated skin. Good for ear infections and insect bites (can use neat where the insect bite has occurred). Geranium is also helpful in repelling ticks. It also helps balance hormones and calms emotions in both animals and humans, good for mares!

GINGER *(Zingiber officinale)*

Ginger is non-toxic, non-irritating and safe to use in small amounts when properly diluted. Good for motion sickness and aids digestion. Effective for pain relief caused by arthritis, dysplasia, strains and sprains.

JUNIPER BERRY *(Juniperus communis)*

Juniper berry essential oil is distilled from the berries. Juniper is antiseptic, antibacterial, toning and detoxifying, useful in all disorders of the skin and blood including psoriasis and eczema. It also helps tissue repair and inhibits infection.

Pet Care with essential oils and their friends

Citrus limon

LAVENDER *(Lavendula angustifolia.)*

Calming and relaxing. The soothing, antiseptic and anti-inflammatory properties of lavender make it valuable for many skin conditions. Lavender will also stimulate the growth of healthy new cells making it effective for cracked skin, eczema, boils, wounds and burns. It is helpful for skin infection as it inhibits the bacteria while soothing the skin. On an emotional level lavender eases anger and frustration.

A "must-have" for dogs and horses!

LEMON *(Citrus limonum)*

Uplifting and relaxing at the same time - good for anxiety. Helps to stimulate the lymphatic system, balances the natural pH in the body and is anti-inflammatory which is useful in the treatment of arthritis and rheumatism.

Pet Care with essential oils and their friends

Origanum majorana

MARJORAM SWEET *(Origanum marjorana)*

Marjoram is calming and a muscle relaxant. A great pain relief for arthritis and general aches and pains. Good for bacterial skin infections, wound care and for repelling insects.

Calming for dogs and horses that are "girl" crazy as it reduces sexual desire (anaphrodisiac).

MYRRH *(Commiphora myrrha)*

Myrrh is extracted from a desert tree that grows in the Middle East. Its thick reddish-brown oil is obtained through extraction and distillation of its resin.

The three wise men knew a thing or two about myrrh as it was widely used by the Egyptians in embalming. Myrrh oil is rejuvenating, fungicidal, anti-inflammatory, antiseptic, cooling and astringent. Is great to use in ointments for wound healing, cuts, abrasions and general skin conditions. Can be used for teething pain in puppies, myrrh also repels ticks

NIAOULI *(Melaleuca quinquenervia or viridflora)*

Niaouli is antihistaminic and a powerful bactericide, a much better choice than tea tree that can be harmful to dogs and cats. Good for ear infections and skin problems caused by allergies.

Rosmarinus officinalis

ORANGE SWEET *(Citrus sinensis)*

Orange is uplifting and stress relieving. Great to add to shampoos for its deodorizing and flea-repelling abilities as well as its lovely fragrance.

PEPPERMINT *(Mentha piperita)*

Peppermint is antispasmodic, stimulates circulation and is insect-repelling. Good for arthritis, dysplasia, sprains and strains. Works well with ginger to treat motion sickness.

Another "must-have" for dogs!

ROSEMARY *(Rosmarinus officinalis)*

Rosemary has been used for skin and hair care for hundreds of years. Due to its rejuvenating effects, rosemary stimulates hair growth and helps produce shiny coats in horses and dogs, it is traditionally used to restore hair loss in humans. Because of its astringent and antiseptic properties, rosemary oil stimulates the circulation and metabolism of the skin.

VALERIAN *(Valeriana officinalis)*

Calming, grounding and sedating. Valerian is good for treating dog separation and noise anxiety.

About Bach Flower Remedies:

Although not essential oils I have used Bach flower remedies successfully on my pets especially Rescue remedy, Rock rose, Crab apple and Agrimony.

AGRIMONY- mental torture behind a cheerful face.
Animals often put on a cheerful face even when in distress in order to please.

CRAB APPLE - the cleansing remedy, also for self-hatred.
I have always used this for skin disorders where there might be fleas or mites, boils and cysts. Acne in humans for example!

ROCK ROSE - terror and fright.

RESCUE REMEDY - This mix was created by Dr. Bach to deal with emergencies and crises - the moments when there is no time to make a proper individual selection of remedies. It can be used to help our pets and ourselves get through any stressful moments.

More can be found out about Bach Flower Remedies at http://www.bachcentre.com/centre/remedies.htm.

Vegetable oils & other ingredients used in the recipes.

In order to achieve the best quality as possible, it is important to use carrier oils that are cold pressed.

ALMOND OIL, SWEET *(Prunus dulcis)*

Sweet almond oil is extracted from the ripe seeds or sweet almonds of the almond tree. There also exists an essential oil from bitter almonds which is never used in treatments because of the risk of prussic acid forming during distillation.

Sweet almond oil contains both mono - and polyunsaturated fatty acids and vitamins (A, B1, B2 and B6). Because, it has small amounts of Vitamin E, it will keep for longer periods of time than other carrier oils and will not easily go rancid. Almond oil penetrates well into the skin, being both nourishing and protecting, it also soothes eczema.

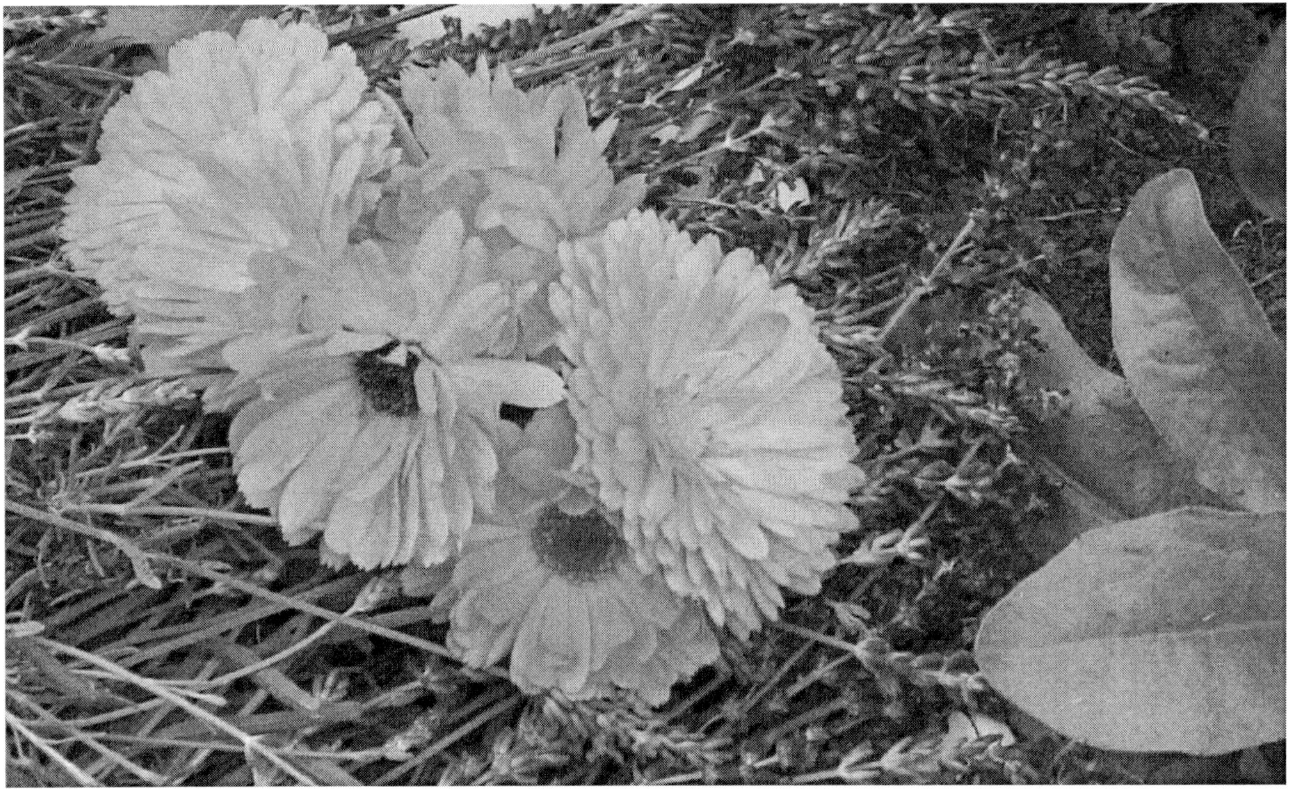

CALENDULA OIL *(Calendula officinalis)*

Calendula, known as pot marigold, is extracted from the flower heads of the plant. Calendula oil is anti-inflammatory and has proved highly successful in the healing of chapped and cracked skin. Because of its amazing healing power, calendula oil has been used in ointments and tinctures throughout Europe and America for hundreds of years.

CORNACOPA *(Decyl glucose)*

Made from re-growable raw materials – glucose derived from corn and fatty alcohols from coconut and palm kernel oils. Although cornacopa has been around for years, the use was previously limited by the lack of a large scale commercial plant. Cornacopa is biodegradable, earth-friendly, orally non-toxic and very mild to the skin and eyes. It can make up to 50% of the shampoo.

GRAPEFRUIT SEED EXTRACT

Is a by-product of the citrus industry, grapefruit seed extract contains vitamin C and glycerin. Grapefruit seed extract is anti-bacterial, anti-microbial, antiseptic, and can be used internally to combat fungus infections. As a result, this makes a natural preservative for creams, lotions and shampoos.

Pet Care with essential oils and their friends

HORSETAIL EXTRACT *(Equisetum arvense)*

Horsetail is an herb that yields a high concentration of silica and other minerals. Silica promotes the re-growth, strength and elasticity of fur.

It is named horsetail because the herb looks like a horsetail

HYDROSOLS/HYDROLATS

Rose, Lavender, Orange blossom, and Lemon Balm when steam distilled, produce hydrosols (hydrolats) which are important in skin care due to their rejuvenating abilities. These waters are antiseptic and astringent as well as being skin - soothing. Beware of purchasing hydrosols that are called "floral waters", as these are usually made with essential oils that have been added to water. A chemical is then added to disperse the essential oil throughout the water.

JOJOBA OIL *(Simmondsia chinensis)*

Jojoba oil is derived from jojoba beans. However, it is technically not an oil but a liquid wax, which, replaced sperm whale oil in the cosmetics industry when the whale became an endangered species. As an added bonus, it is an environmental aid, as planting it saves arid land from becoming desert. Jojoba is good for dry skin, psoriasis and eczema. High quality Jojoba oil is without colour or odour and has a long shelf life, making it ideal for use in creams, oils and hair conditioners.

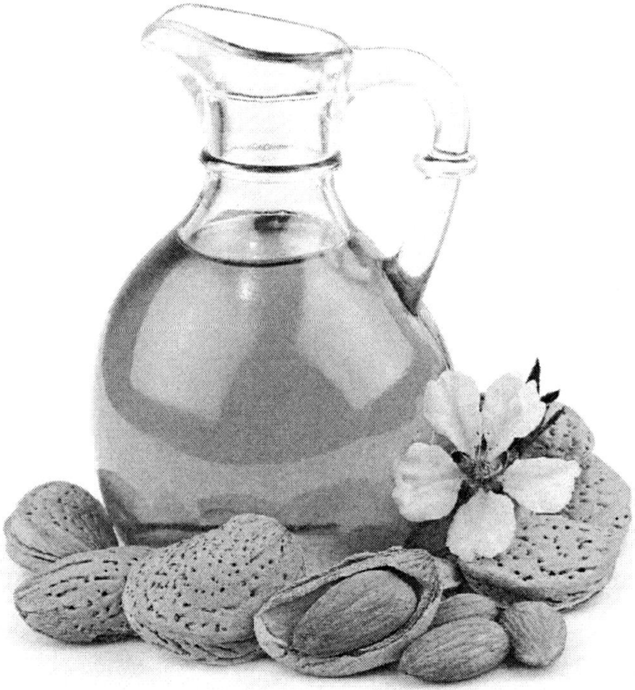

NETTLE EXTRACT *(Urtica dioica)*

Nettle is used in shampoo to control dandruff and gives shine to the fur.

WHEAT PROTEIN

This adds protection for the skin and hair as it moisturises and softens. Wheat protein strengthens the elasticity of the hair and repairs damage to the hair especially hair that has been overly processed and coloured. When added to the shampoo, the wheat protein can turn the shampoo into an all-in-one shampoo and conditioner.

SEAWEED EXTRACT *(Sargassum Fillipendula, Hypnea musciformis, Gelidiella acerosa)*

Marine algae are full of easy to absorb proteins, vitamins, minerals and lipids that have the ability to repair and protect the skin and fur.

WITCH HAZEL *(Hamamelis virginiana)*

Witch hazel is distilled from the leaves, flowers and bark of the hamamelis tree. It has healing, anti-inflammatory and astringent qualities; is particularly helpful as a poultice on bruises.

Other oils such as sunflower, evening primrose, hemp seed, olive, grape seed etc. can be used in pet care. More information about these oils can be found in the Creamy Craft of Cosmetic Making book.

Pet Care with essential oils and their friends

CHAPTER TWO

Why make your own pet care products?

People are drawn to making pet care products for a host of different reasons. Some people have dogs that are prone to allergic reactions or have skin conditions due for example to the commercial shampoo that is being used. Others simply want to try a more natural and holistic approach to taking care of their pets, using pure and environmentally-friendly ingredients.

In this chapter you will find simple recipes on making shampoos and pet care products that have been tried and tested on humans.

Tools of the Trade

For making shampoos, conditioners and ointments you will need the following equipment:

- 1 double boiler, (glass bowl placed over a pot of boiling water)
- 1 stainless steel saucepan.
- A stirring spoon and measuring spoons.
- A measuring jug 1 litre.
- Weighing scale.
- Empty bottles for shampoos and treatment oils. Spray bottles for deodorants and bug sprays and glass jars for ointments.
- Labels and a waterproof felt-tip pen.

Clean all equipment in boiling water or at least wash them well with hot soapy water; rinse well and dry. It is best to use these utensils only for making cosmetics and not to prepare or store food in them.

Cautions when making products:

- Pay attention when heating oil:
- If the phone or doorbell goes, remove pan from heat. Small amounts of oils like this can overheat in seconds if left unattended.
- Do not overheat the oils.
- Keep young children and pets out of the way.
- Keep a bottle of Lavender nearby in the event of being burnt by oil.
- Remove any oil or cream split on the floor or you could end up looking like this!

Shampoo

First of all we'll start off with shampoo. Shampoo is one of the worst offenders regarding the use of ingredients such as sodium laurel sulphate, anti-freeze, artificial fragrances and preservatives etc. These ingredients are not just harmful to humans and dogs but can cause allergic reactions as well. The following shampoo recipe does not contain any of the above products, is environmentally friendly and can be safely used in fresh water lakes.

Experimental Basic Shampoo

Ingredients

    100 ml Distilled water

    50 ml Cornacopa

    ¼ tsp. Xanthan gum

    1/8 tsp. Vegetable glycerin

    1/8 tsp. Wheat protein

Preservative

    1 drop Grapefruit seed extract

Method:

1. Heat the water and sprinkle the Xanthan Gum onto the water and stir.
2. When the Xanthan Gum has dissolved in the water (I often use a handheld blender to quicken the process), mix in the Wheat protein, Vegetable glycerin and Grapefruit seed extract.
3. Gently fold in the cornacopa.
4. Enhance with goodies such as essential oils (for this recipe, use a total of 4 drops essential oil/s) and Vitamin E.
5. Bottle and label.

Shampoo Base

Ingredients

- **800 ml** Distilled water
- **100 ml** Rose or neroli hydrolat (floral water)
- **2 dsp/20 ml** Xanthan Gum (fine meshed)
- **3 tsp/15ml** Vegetable glycerin
- **1 dsp/10ml** Wheat protein
- **500ml** Cornacopa
- **1 capsule** vitamin E
- **10 drops** pro-vitamin B5
- **½ tsp.** Grapefruit seed extract

Method

1. Heat the waters in a stainless steel saucepan and sprinkle the xanthan gum onto the water, stir in.
2. When the xanthan gum has dissolved in the water (a hand held blender quickens the process), mix in the wheat protein, vegetable glycerin and grapefruit seed extract.
3. Gently fold in the cornacopa and add essential oils, herbal extracts and vitamins.

Doggie Shampoo

I first developed this shampoo for a friend's dog who was suffering from itchy skin after using commercial dog shampoo. It has now become a favourite of some of my customers as well as dog groomers because not only is it soothing to dogs with sensitive skins, but makes them smell good as well.

Great on horses and humans as well!

To 250ml of the shampoo base add the following goodies:

2 drops roman chamomile essential oil

8 drops lavender essential oil

3 drops geranium essential oil

For cats: use ¼ the amount of essential oils.

Sparkle and Shine Shampoo

To 250ml of the shampoo base add the following goodies:

5 drops sweet orange essential oil

3 drops lavender essential oil

3 drops geranium essential oil

2 drops rosemary essential oil

4 drops nettle extract

2 drops horsetail extract

For cats: use ¼ the amount of essential oils.

Chamomile Shampoo

This shampoo is especially helpful for eczema or psoriasis.

To 250ml of the shampoo base add the following goodies:

5 drops roman chamomile essential oil

4 drops nettle extract

3 drops agrimony Bach flower remedy

3 drops crab apple Bach flower remedy

Conditioners

Fur that is dry tangles easily and might be in need of extra nourishment. This conditioner balances the pH balance of the hair which will result in a shiny coat.

Experimental Basic Conditioner

Ingredients

Waxes and Oils:

10gms Conditioning wax emulsifier

Waters:

100 ml Distilled water

Preservative:

1 large drop Grapefruit seed extract

Method:

1. Heat up the water in a stainless steel saucepan.
2. Add the emulsifying wax to the hot water and heat until all the wax has melted.
3. Remove the pot from the heat source.
4. Stir until cool.
5. Add the Grapefruit seed extract, goodies and essential oils.
6. Bottle and label.

Jojoba Conditioner

Rich in ingredients which supply nutrients to the hair. Seaweed and Nettle extract help repair damaged hair. Jojoba oil coats the hair shaft to provide additional protection.

Ingredients

Waxes and oils:

50gms Conditioning wax emulsifier

Waters:

400 ml Distilled water

100 ml Neroli or Rose hydrolat

½ **tsp**. Citric acid

½ **tsp.** Seaweed extract

Preservative:

    1 large drop Grapefruit seed extract

Goodies and Essential Oils:

    ¼ **tsp**. Jojoba or sweet almond Oil

    1 drop Vitamin E

    3 drops Nettle extract

    1 drop D-Panthenol (B5)

    10 drops Roman chamomile or Lavender essential oil

For cats: use ¼ the amount of essential oils.

Method:

    1. Heat the waters, Seaweed extract and Citric acid.

    2. Add emulsifying wax to the hot water and heat until completely melted.

    3. Remove the pot from the heat source. Stir until cool.

    4. Add the Grapefruit seed extract, Jojoba oil, Vitamin E, herbal extracts and essential oils.

To Use: After shampooing, apply a small amount and rinse.

Conditioning Oil

Conditions the skin and fur and helps repel fleas

Ingredients

Oils:

    50ml Sweet almond oil

Goodies and Essential Oils:

    1 drop Vitamin E

    5 drops Lavender essential oil

    1 drop Cedarwood essential oil

To use: Massage approximately 5ml over the coat and into the skin twice weekly.

CHAPTER THREE
Common disorders
Arthritis and Rheumatism (aches and pains)

Arthritis is inflammation of the bones, whereas Rheumatism is inflammation of the muscles and can strike at any age, although it usually happens more frequently as both humans and our furry friends get older.

If you suspect that your pet is suffering from one or more of the symptoms mentioned in the list below for more than two weeks, take him to your veterinarian for an evaluation, which will involve a physical exam and possibly X-rays. In fact, arthritis is one of the most common sources of chronic pain that veterinarians treat.

Signs that your dog may have arthritis or rheumatism:

- Favouring a limb
- Difficulty sitting or standing
- Sleeps a lot

- Seems to have stiff or sore joints
- Hesitancy to jump, run or climb stairs
- Weight gain
- Decreased activity or less interest in play
- Attitude or behaviour changes
- Is less alert

If your dog happens to have one or more of any the above symptoms, it might just be general aches and pains! Try changing your pets diet and exercising it more, apply the arthritis or aches and pains blend to the sore area twice daily.

You never know, this might just alleviate the problem and postpone arthritis and rheumatism in the future!

If your pet is diagnosed with arthritis then the treatment of canine arthritis is similar to that of human osteoarthritis.

Therapies may include:

- Healthy diet and exercise to help maintain proper weight.
- Working with your veterinarian to find a drug treatment that helps relieve the pain.
- Over-the-counter pet treatments, such as pills or food containing Omega fatty acids have shown to help relieve the symptoms of arthritis.
- Application of essential oils mixed in carrier oils. See Recipes and Treatments.

Eczema

Eczema is an acute or chronic inflammation of the skin showing scales or crusts. Not infectious, it itches and burns. Eczema can cause extreme discomfort for an animal, and flare ups can often be triggered by fleas, allergic reactions and environmental factors. This condition affects cats, dogs and horses of all breeds and is most common in animals with sensitive skin.

With most types of eczema the following symptoms may be noted with regards to your pet:

- Itching that may range from moderate to severe in certain areas

- Lesions on areas of skin that become sparsely haired (back of paws, abdomen, muzzle and lips).
- Inflamed areas that may bleed when scratched or ooze watery fluids.
- Blistering.
- Cracked, painful skin.
- Persistent licking of a particular area
- Persistent scratching of a particular area.
- The appearance of red painful-looking sores, often overnight.
- Scaly, rough or oozing areas on the skin, usually accompanied by hair loss.

Psoriasis

Psoriasis is a chronic inflammatory disease. It is not infectious and somewhat resembles eczema. It is recognized by elevated reddish patches covered by thick, dry, scaly patches of silver coloured scabs. When these scales are lifted, tiny bleeding points may be noticed. Its cause is unknown; food and nerves may be partially responsible. Again as with eczema, environmental factors and allergies may be a contributory cause of psoriasis.

RECIPES and TREATMENTS

Healing Ointment

This recipe works well on chronic psoriasis, eczema, helps heal sores, cuts and rashes.

Ingredients

Waxes and oils:

    8gms Beeswax

    ½ **tsp**. Shea butter

    30ml Sweet almond oil

    15ml Calendula oil

Goodies and Essential Oils:

    1 drop Vitamin E

    2 drops Roman chamomile

    2 drops Lavender

    1 drop Myrrh

    1 drop Helichrysm

Method:

- Sterilize all utensils and worktop.
- Melt the beeswax, shea butter and oils in a double boiler.
- When the wax and oils are completely melted, remove from the heat.
- Add the essential oils and vitamin E.
- Immediately pour into sterilized jars while still liquid.

To Apply: Gently apply a small amount to the affected area as often as necessary.

Eczema oil

To 30ml of sweet almond oil, add the following essential oils:

5 drops Bergamot

5 drops Geranium

5 drops Juniper berry

5 drops Lavender

To Apply: Use a few drops twice daily, gently apply to the affected area.

Anti-stress

To 50ml of sweet almond oil add the following essential oils:

12 drops Clary sage

10 drops Sweet Orange

3 drops Lavender

To Apply: Use a few drops twice daily, gently massage the muscles on the back and neck.

Aches and Pains

To 50ml of sweet almond oil, add the following essential oils:

8 drops Eucalyptus

8 drops Sweet Marjoram

8 drops Lavender

To Apply: Use a few drops twice daily, gently massage into your dog's sore joints or painful areas.

Arthritis and Rheumatism

To 15ml of sweet almond oil, add the following essential oils:

6 drops Helichrysm

4 drops Peppermint

3 drops Ginger

2 drops Valerian

To Apply: Use a few drops twice daily, gently massage into your dog's sore joints or painful areas caused by arthritis.

Bad Odour Spray

On a bad rainy day, the "doggy smell" may be more profound than ever. Use this spray to get rid of that smell!

Ingredients

5ml Cider vinegar or rose water

95ml Distilled water

Essential Oils:

10 drops Lavender

6 drops Peppermint

6 drops Sweet orange

3 drops Eucalyptus radiata

Method:

1. Mix the essential oil and cider vinegar in a spray bottle, shake gently.

2. Add the water.

To Apply: Shake before using, Cover your dog's face and eyes with one hand and spray directly onto your dog's body especially the paws, legs and under the belly. You can also spray the room and your pets bedding with this blend.

Fur tonic

The following Fur tonic helps restore fur loss and promotes a shiny coat.

Ingredients

    50ml of witch hazel

Essential Oils:

    3 drops Cedarwood (cats and small dogs 1 drop)

    5 drops Juniper berry (cats and small dogs 1 drop)

    10 drops Rosemary (cats and small dogs 4 drops)

Method:

    1. Mix the essential oil and witch hazel in a spray bottle, shake gently.

To Apply: Shake before using, Cover your pet's face and eyes with one hand and spray a small amount to the skin on the affected area morning and night. Massage the area by gluing fingertips to skin and rotating the skin over the bone.

Caution: Because of the rosemary essential oil, do not use on animals or humans prone to seizures or epilepsy!

Bug Spray

For both dogs and horses. This insect repellent will help eliminate fleas, repel ticks, mosquitoes and black flies. Great for humans too!

Ingredients

5ml Cider vinegar

95ml Distilled water

Essential Oils:

8 drops Eucalyptus radiata or citronella

6 drops Sweet Orange

4 drops Lavender

4 drops Peppermint

3 drops Geranium

1 drop Cedarwood

Method:

1. Mix the essential oils and cider vinegar in a spray bottle, shake gently.
2. Add the water.

To Apply: Shake before using, Cover your dog's face and eyes with one hand and spray directly onto your dog's body especially the paws, legs and under the belly.

Hot Spot Itch relief Spray

This spray quickly calms and relieves painful hot spots and soothes itchy, raw, irritated skin.

Ingredients

5ml Rose or Neroli water

45ml Distilled water

Essential Oils:

6 drops Roman Chamomile

4 drops Lavender

2 drops Peppermint

Method:

1. Mix the essential oils and rose or neroli water in a spray bottle, shake gently.

2. Add the water.

To Apply: Shake before using, Cover your pet's face and eyes with one hand and use wherever needed.

CHAPTER FOUR

Designing a Blend

You can follow the recipes given above, but sometimes it is necessary to design your own treatments. For example, let's take look at Benson. Benson is a 9 year old dog and is acting stressed, not acting like himself. The family have just moved and he has also since the move started to lose fur in his lower back! He also seems to be suffering from mild aches and pains, he is after all 9 years old!

The holistic therapist looks at the whole picture and creates a blend for both the fur loss, the stress from the move, and the aches and pains. Treating both the physical and emotional conditions.

It is important to remember blending a whole orchestra into one blend is not the answer to all our prayers. Each blend has a purpose, whether it be uplifting or sedating or working on the hormonal system etc. at the same time as a blend has a specific path, it is also aiding in the whole health of the individual. This is due to many levels Aromatherapy works on and the dynamism of each essential oil.

Synergy

"The action of two or more substances, organs, or organisms to achieve an effect of which each is individually incapable".

"From the Greek word sunergos meaning working together: working in harmony".

The concept of synergy is of notable importance in the Art of Aromatherapy. As you begin to blend you will recognize how essential oils combine with one another to create a unified fragrance or odour. When they are not unified, you will smell a fragrance of disharmony.

Synergy occurs when there is complete harmony. Take for example, an orchestra playing a piece of music, at times the music will be wild with movement. Moving here and there and back again, going high and low, increasing and decreasing in dynamics. You will hear flutes, and then violins will join in, suddenly the drums will begin and off again the music whirls. Then in one momentous second the orchestra is in complete harmony, there is no differentiation between violin, flute, drum or bass. The orchestra is playing as one and somehow this moves us deeply in that second. This is wholeness. This is synergy.

Synergy is when the whole is greater than the sum of its parts.

How do we achieve this with essential oils?

- Practice the art of blending – we all make mistakes, it is a natural experience. Learning from the mistakes means noting the number of drops we used, what could you have used less of, more of, etc……

- Know the essential oils you are working with before setting out.

- Have a clear goal for the blend without making this an all-around blend, energy can easily get scattered and not have a focus. If you need a blend for two opposing problems, then make two blends, instead of trying to have one blend do everything. Research shows that more than 5 oils is counterproductive.

- Remember Lavender is the best synergizer, so you can add even a drop to a blend to help increase the benefits of the given blend.

All of these small details add to the synergistic property of a blend.

Blending

Blending is the Art of Aromatherapy and takes time, knowledge, intuition and attention to become an expert at. The concept of synergy plays an important role in blending.

Research on essential oils has shown that a blend of 3 to 4 essential oils produces greater healing powers than they do when used singly. However, a blend of more than 5 essential oils has no more marked effect and hence is not necessary.

The standard dilution for an aromatherapy blend is 0.5% (for cats and small dogs) - 2.5% (large dogs and horses) which is equivalent to 3 to 15 drops per 30ml of carrier oil. A more typical medical or treatment blend is 1% to 5% which is equal to 6 to 30 drops per 30ml of carrier oil. Typically in an individual treatment 1 (for Cats) – 10 (for horses) drops is blended into a carrier oil and the complete blend is applied whether it be the whole body or a part thereof.

Usually we are aiming for a well-rounded blend although in some instances it may be appropriate to have a top note blend (ie. In the case of a down, depressed, or lethargic pet), and other times it may be necessary to have a base note blend (ie. In the case of a pet who is highly strung and needs to be grounded, relaxed or sedated).

Aromatic Blending

Each blend is made up of 1 - 3 essential oil/s. The following is a guide to creating effective blends.

The first condition – The first condition is perhaps the most important as it will guide your choice for the second and third. I call the oil from the first condition the **Core essential oil**, as it deals with the core issue or concern of the client.

The second condition – The second condition is to support the Core and is called the **Support essential oil.**

The third condition – The third condition is chosen to create a well-rounded blend and hence I call this one the **Rounder essential oil.**

#1 **Core oil (1st condition)**

#2 **Support oil (2nd condition)**

#3 **Rounding oil (3rd condition)**

If you choose three oils then these would be support and rounding in relation to the core oil.

Now to build upon this a little more. The core essential oil may be physical or emotional and the support oil may be physical or emotional. The rounding essential oil can be used as an emotional oil to aid the blend in its aroma and appeal or, if an emotional issue has been used for the core condition, can be for another physical condition.

Top, Middle and Base Notes
All of the essential oils come under one of three categories:

Top, Middle and Base

We use these categories for blending factors.

When used in perfume the first smell picked up is the top note. As the perfume heats up the base note comes out.

Which is why, when buying perfume it is better to apply then wait to see how the chemistry evolves between you and the aromatic compounds. When making aromatherapy perfume blends the same thing occurs. I have often mixed a perfume blend, not enjoyed the aroma at first put it away and left it to mature. 6 months later smelt it again and loved it.

One way of categorizing an essential oil into top, middle and base is based on where the essential oil is extracted from in the plant. (Not always written in stone though)!

Top notes – Leaves, blossom and fruit of trees. i.e. orange, lemon, eucalyptus, and niaouli.

Middle notes – Bushes and herbs. i.e. rosemary, lavender, geranium and juniper berry.

Base notes – Bark/wood of trees, resins, rhizomes, and roots. i.e. cedarwood, ginger and valerian.

Top Notes	Most stimulating and uplifting. They are light fragrant oils that are often used for acute problems and evaporate the fastest.
Middle Notes	Are calming and stimulating. In other words – balancing. Usually the 'doers', effecting physical body, the metabolism, digestion, menstruation etc.
Base Notes	Relaxing and grounding, sedative and relaxing. Heavy, strong smelling oils that are often used for chronic problems and the slowest to evaporate.

The Art of Blending

There are many different techniques used for mixing and blending. Two of the most common ways are with:

- **Inner Knowledge**
- **Cross referencing**

1. Inner knowledge

Using your pet's inner knowledge is a technique used to determine the essential oils best for the client by using your pet's innate intelligence.

A selection of essential oils, usually around 6, is chosen based on the conditions. The therapist (yourself) holds each bottle of essential oil close to the nose of the patient ie. cat, dog, or horse. Follow the guidelines on the chapter **using essential oils on cats, dogs and horses** for this particular art on page 13.

To calculate the amount of drops, use the table on page 77.

2. Cross Referencing

Choose from your consultation techniques the main condition (core), 2nd condition (support), and 3rd condition (rounder).

Check there is a relationship between analysis and conditions treated.

Make sure your cross reference is complete, filling in the names of all the essential oils from the condition in the therapeutic cross reference chart, even if they are not available in your practitioner box. Make a note on your record card to indicate if the oils that would have been used are not available. The number of drops of each essential oil used must be shown on the record card.

Here is an example cross-reference chart where the Benson has stress and anxiety from moving, has unexplained fur loss and also suffers aches and pains. The most important condition is the 'main condition' and all the oils are chosen from this section.

However, if we reference the oils that treat the other two conditions into the main condition, we will have a unique blend of oils that treats every condition.

Main condition (Core)			Second condition			Third condition		
Stress, anxiety			**Fur loss**			**Aches and pains**		
Top	Middle	Base	Top	Middle	Base	Top	Middle	Base
Bergamot	Camomile	Cedarwood		Rosemary		Eucalyptus	Camomile	Ginger
Clary sage	Geranium	Frankincense					Geranium	Helichrysm
Lemon	Juniper	Helichrysm					Juniper	
Orange	Lavender	Myrrh					Lavender	
	Marjoram	Valerian					Marjoram	
	Peppermint						Rosemary	
	Rosemary							

Below is the 'main condition' column of oils. To denote that the oil is also in the second condition (Fur loss) an F is put by each oil. To denote that the oil is also in the third condition (Aches and pains) an A is put by each oil.

\multicolumn{3}{c}{**Stress - anxiety**}		
Bergamot	Chamomile **A**	Cedarwood
Clary sage	Geranium **A**	Helichrysm **A**
Lemon	Lavender **A**	Myrrh
Orange	Juniper **A**	Valerian
	Peppermint	Frankincense
	Marjoram **A**	
	Rosemary **A and F**	

For a synergistic blend ideally use 1 top, 1 middle and 1 base note, but not always so!

In blending whether for treatments or in the making of perfumes, we use more top note drops than base note drops *(see chart opposite).*

To calculate the drops, use the following table:

Information on 'Notes'	Conditions 1 + 2 + 3	Conditions 1 + 2	Conditions 1 + 3
Top Notes Stimulating and uplifting (Aroma lasts up to 24 hours)	4 drops	3 drops	2 drops
Middle Notes Affects most body systems and general metabolism (Aroma lasts 2 to 3 days)	3 drops	2 drops	1 drop
Base Notes Relaxing and grounding (Aroma still around after 1 week)	1 drop	1 drop	1 drop

*For cutting adjustments: Always cut everything by 1/3 or 1/2.

It would be written on the client record card as:

In this case I chose 2 middle and 1 base note: **Essential oils chosen with drops used based on the formula above:** Rosemary 3, geranium 1 and Helichrysm 1 = 5 drops, added to 10mls of Sweet almond oil.

Rosemary treats all 3 conditions, Geranium treats stress and aches and pains and Helichrysm treats stress and aches and pains.

For a dog or horse, use the whole 10ml amount for daily treatment. For a cat or small dog, simply use 2 to 5ml of the completed mix.

This blend is calculated for a treatment blend. Oils that treat all three conditions should be chosen if possible. If not, then concentrate on conditions 1 and 2. After all, condition 3 is of least importance or it would not occupy this position. Once the essential oils and carriers are chosen, pour the correct amount of carrier into a measuring cup and then add the essential oils. Mix the blend with your finger – you are part of the treatment!

If you are using three oils, as in the example above, then add one drop of each oil first and let Benson smell the blend and get his approval before using the full dosage.

For general massage use times the above blend by 2 to 4 (depending on the % used) and add up to 50ml of carrier oil/s.

Tables

Mixing %

CLIENT	PERCENTAGE	TOTAL NUMBER OF DROPS
Cats and Elderly pets	1/8 % - ½ %	1/4 drop in 10ml carrier oil 1 drop in 10ml carrier oil
Small/medium dogs	1% - 3%	2 drops in 10ml carrier oil 6 drops in 10ml carrier oil
Large dogs and Horses	1% - 5%	2 drops in 10ml carrier oil 10 drops in 10ml carrier oil

Proper Measurement

Ounces	Drams	Spoons	cc's	ml's
1/8	=1	=1/2 tsp.	= 2	= 2
1/4	=2	=1 tsp.	= 5	= 5
1/3	=3	=1 dsp.	= 10	= 10
1/2	=4	=1 tbsp.	= 15	= 15
1	=8	=2 tbsp.	=30	= 30
4	=32	=4 tbsp.	=120	=120

Therapeutic Cross Reference Chart

For the essential oils mentioned in this book.

Top Notes		Middle Notes		Base Notes	
Bergamot	Ber	Chamomile	Cam	Cedarwood	C/W
Carrot seed	Car	Geranium	Ger	Frankincense	Frank
Clary Sage	C/S	Juniper	Jun	Ginger	Gin
Eucalyptus	Euc	Lavender	Lav	Helicrysm	Heli
Lemon	Lem	Marjoram sweet	Mar	Myrrh	Myr
Niaouli	Nia	Peppermint	P/M	Valerian	Val
Orange sweet	Ora	Rosemary	R/M		

Digestive disorders

Problem	Top Notes	Middle Notes	Base Notes
Colic	Bergamot	Juniper Lavender Peppermint	
Constipation	Lemon Orange Sweet	Chamomile Juniper Marjoram Rosemary	Ginger
Diarrhoea	Eucalyptus Lemon Orange Sweet	Chamomile Geranium Juniper Lavender Marjoram Peppermint Rosemary	Ginger Myrrh

Problem	Top Notes	Middle Notes	Base Notes
Flatulence (gas)	Bergamot	Juniper Lavender Peppermint Rosemary	Ginger Myrrh
Loss of appetite	Bergamot	Chamomile Juniper	Ginger
Vomiting	Lemon	Chamomile Peppermint	Ginger

Head and Neck Disorders

Problem	Top Notes	Middle Notes	Base Notes
Ear problems	Bergamot Niaouli	Chamomile Geranium Lavender	
Colds	Eucalyptus Lemon Niaouli	Geranium Juniper Lavender Marjoram Peppermint Rosemary	Cedarwood Frankincense
Teething - in young puppies			Myrrh

Muscular & Joint Disorders

Problem	Top Notes	Middle Notes	Base Notes
Aches and Pains	Eucalyptus	Chamomile Geranium Juniper Lavender Marjoram Peppermint Rosemary	Ginger Helichrysm
Arthritis	Bergamot Eucalyptus Lemon Niaouli	Chamomile Geranium Juniper Lavender Marjoram Rosemary	Cedarwood Frankincense Ginger Myrh

Problem	Top Notes	Middle Notes	Base Notes
Rheumatism	Eucalyptus Lemon Niaouli	Chamomile Lavender Marjoram Rosemary Juniper	Ginger Helichrysm
Sprains/Strains	Eucalyptus	Chamomile Lavender Marjoram Peppermint Rosemary	Ginger Helichrysm Valerian

Fur and Skin Disorders

Problem	Top Notes	Middle Notes	Base Notes
Abscesses/Boils	Bergamot Eucalyptus Lemon Niaouli	Chamomile Geranium Juniper Lavender Peppermint Rosemary	Helichrysm Myrrh
Allergies (skin)	Eucalyptus	Chamomile Lavender	Helichrysm
Eczema	Bergamot Carrot seed Eucalyptus Niaouli	Chamomile Geranium Juniper Lavender	Cedarwood Frankincense Helichrysm Myrrh

Problem	Top Notes	Middle Notes	Base Notes
Allergy prone or sensitive skin	Carrot seed	Chamomile Lavender	Helichrysm
Fur loss		Rosemary	
Inflamed skin	Clary sage	Chamomile Geranium Lavender Peppermint	Frankincense Helichrysm Myrrh
Bruises		Chamomile Lavender Marjoram Rosemary	Ginger Myrrh
Burns	Eucalyptus Niaouli	Chamomile Geranium Lavender	

Problem	Top Notes	Middle Notes	Base Notes
Dry, itchy & cracked skin	Carrot seed	Chamomile Geranium Lavender	Myrrh
Psoriasis	Bergamot Carrot seed Niaouli	Chamomile Geranium Lavender	Cedarwood Helichrysm
Fungal skin infections	Bergamot Niaouli	Geranium Peppermint Rosemary	Helichrysm

Mental/Emotional Symptoms

Problem	Top Notes	Middle Notes	Base Notes
Abandonment both physical and emotional	Carrot seed		
Anger		Chamomile Lavender Peppermint	
Anxiety	Bergamot Clary sage Lemon Orange	Chamomile Geranium Juniper Lavender Marjoram Peppermint Rosemary	Cedarwood Frankincense Helichrysm Myrrh Valerian
Balancing - emotions & hormones	Clary sage	Geranium	

Problem	Top Notes	Middle Notes	Base Notes
Change - adjusting to	Clary sage		
Compulsiveness	Clary sage		
Depression	Bergamot Clary sage Niaouli Orange	Chamomile Geranium Lavender Juniper Marjoram Rosemary	Frankincense Helichrysm
Emotional stress	Clary sage	Juniper Lavender Marjoram	

Problem	Top Notes	Middle Notes	Base Notes
Fear • Acute • Of People • Rigid with • Of unknown origin		Geranium Lavendar Geranium Lavender	
Grief		Marjoram	
Hostility	Clary sage	Marjoram	
Hyperactivity	Clary sage	Lavender	
Hypersensitivity		Peppermint	
Hysteria	Orange	Chamomile Lavender Marjoram Peppermint	Cedarwood Frankincense Helichrysm Valerian

Problem	Top Notes	Middle Notes	Base Notes
Impatience		Chamomile Lavender	
Impulsiveness		Chamomile	
Insecurity		Lavender	Frankincense
Insomnia	Clary sage Orange	Chamomile Juniper Lavender Marjoram	Valerian
Instability		Geranium	
Irritability	Bergamot Clary sage Orange	Chamomile Lavender Marjoram	

Problem	Top Notes	Middle Notes	Base Notes
Loneliness		Marjoram	
Moodiness, mood swings	Eucalyptus	Geranium Lavender	
Nightmares		Lavender	
Obstinacy	Orange		
Palpitations, nervous		Lavender	
Panic attacks	Clary sage	Lavender	
Resentment	Clary sage Lemon		
Sadness	Orange	Marjoram	
Shyness		Peppermint	

Problem	Top Notes	Middle Notes	Base Notes
Stage/Show fright		Lavender	
Stress general - see anxiety			
Sudden stress		Junpier Lavender Marjoram Peppermint	Frankincense Valerian
Tantrums in pets	Clary sage	Chamomile	Valerian
Tension, nervous	Clary sage	Chamomile Geranium Juniper Lavender Marjoram	Cedarwood Frankincense Valerian

Misc. Disorders

Problem	Top Notes	Middle Notes	Base Notes
Anaphrodisiac - reduces sexual desire		Marjoram	
Flea-repelling	Eucalyptus	Marjoram Peppermint	Cedarwood
Tick-repelling		Geranium Marjoram Peppermint	Cedarwood Myrrh
Insect bites		Geranium	
Motion sickness		Peppermint	Ginger

CHAPTER FIVE

Starting Your Pet Care Business

How to Start Your Home Based Pet Care Business

The pet care industry is a booming business. Everywhere one turns, there is a product being advertised or marketed promising wonderful results. From an entrepreneurial standpoint, investing in a business with a large demand is a great way to become your own boss. Paired with the convenience of working from home, can also be an effective method of generating additional income every month.

Making your own pet care products is not difficult and can be done in your house with basic ingredients.

Instructions

- Decide on the pet care products you would like to sell. Doing so will allow you to select and research a clear target market to pursue. Also, determine whether you will sell commercial products sold in stores or an earth-friendly organic line.

- Create a business name and company logo to use on packaging materials. You may register your establishment name, as well as the form of operation, such as an individual, partnership or corporation. You may also need to obtain your seller's permit and insurance, other required licenses to fully operate your business.

- Choose a room where you will work to create your products, it could be your kitchen or you might have a spare room that can be your "creation" room. Here you can store your equipment and ingredients as well as formulate and make your products.

- Buy the equipment, ingredients and containers necessary to manufacture your products.
- Create your labels and decide on your presentation package.
- Create marketing materials including business cards, brochures and fliers to help promote your pet care line. If you want to sell your products online, create a website that highlights products and ordering information.
- Samples are a good idea to give out to potential clients.
- Work out a pricing structure depending on your market.
- Market your business locally. Create fliers advertising your business or contract a graphic designer or printing service to create a catalog of your merchandise. Distribute your fliers at local dog grooming centres, libraries, work, and college bulletin boards. Approach your local vet! Hosting home pet parties is a great way to market your products to animal loving friends, family and neighbors. Take out an advertisement in your local newspaper to reach a wider audience.

- Rent a small merchant booth at a local farmer's market, swap meet or community festival. Providing samples of your pet care line and a catalog detailing your inventory is an effective way to gain recognition with your community.

Tips and Warnings

- Be careful when working with making products to always keep a clean and safe environment
- As with any business, speak to a lawyer and accountant to make sure all legal and financial obligations are met.

Ingredients needed before making the products presented in this book.

- Sweet almond oil ½ kg
- Beeswax 25gms
- Calendula oil 50ml
- Citric acid 1 tsp.
- Cornacopa ½ kg
- Distilled water
- Grapefruit seed extract 25gms
- Hair conditioning wax emulsifier 100gms
- Hydrolats (Rose or Neroli water) 200ml
- Horsetail extract 50gms
- Jojoba oil 50ml
- Nettle extract 50gms
- Seaweed extract 10gms
- Shea butter 20gms
- Wheat protein 50gms

- Witch hazel 100ml
- Vegetable glycerin 50ml
- Vitamin B5 25gms
- Vitamin E 25gms
- Xanthan Gum 25gms
- Essential oils: Bergamot, Carrot seed, Clary sage, Eucalyptus radiata, Lemon, Niaouli, Orange sweet, Chamomile Roman, Geranium, Juniper, Lavender, Marjoram sweet, Peppermint, Rosemary, Cedarwood, Frankincense, Ginger, Helichrysm, Myrrh and Valerian.
- Empty containers including: Plastic bottles for shampoos and conditioners, 50ml bottles for treatment blends, glass jars for ointments and spritz bottles.

Final Word

By using the essential oils and their friends in their many applications such as shampoo, bug sprays and doggy deodorants. I hope that both you and your furry friends live a healthier, happier longer and aromatic life!

In memory of Tier

If you enjoyed this book, here are some other books by the author.

The Creamy Craft of Cosmetic Making *with essential oils and their friends,* **1996, 2011** as well as being a cream and lotion making book, studies the use of essential oils and carrier oils in skin, body and hair care products. Also included is treatments for body care especially cellulite and fat reduction, along with a diet and plan of action. Care of the skin is covered including treatments for stretch marks, varicose veins and aches and pains.

The Complete Book of Lipsticks, 2013 contains everything you wanted to know about lipsticks with historical titbits, and ingredients used in natural lipsticks.

Learn how to make organic lipsticks with healthy and all natural ingredients including using essential oils in your lipsticks. The book also includes how to start your own cosmetic making business. Recipes included are Baby pink, Bella rosa, Spice, Rudy, Coco la creme, Chocolate kisses, (made with real chocolate) and Goth.

The Baby Boomers Beauty Bible, 2011 Contains everything you need to know on how to make a complete skin, body and hair care line including: Hair shampoos and conditioners, skin care products including cleansers, toners and moisturisers, body lotions, hand and foot care products and lip balms. Anti-ageing, Neck firming, Rosacea and various skin care treatments using essential oils and other natural ingredients are covered. Also included are recipes for natural sun screens, insect repellents and deodorants. Presented with witty and straight forward advice for body care that includes suggestions to soothe the soul and stimulate the mind.

For more recipes, check out the following websites:

www.makeyourownlipstick.com

www.classicaromatherapy.com

www.holisticperfume.com

www.thequeenofcosmetics.com

www.aromashoppe.com

www.makeyourowncosmetics.org

We offer Diploma Courses in Cosmetic Making, Aromatherapy and Holistic Skin Care.

We also carry all the ingredients necessary for making your own products.

Canada

The Aroma shoppe Ltd.,
Toronto, Ontario

E-mail: janbenham@gmail.com

www.makeyourowncosmetics.org

Great Britain

The Aroma shoppe Ltd.,
Nottingham

E-mail: janbenham@gmail.com

www.aromashoppe.com

About the Author

Jan Benham is the President of the Institute of Aromatherapy and Aroma Shoppe. She is a holistic therapist, practicing and teaching for over twenty five years.

Jan is a fellow of the Society of Health and Beauty Therapists UK, member of the International Federation of Holistic Therapists UK, member of the International Federation of Professional Aromatherapists, UK, a Registered Aromatherapy Health Practitioner with the Canadian Examining Board of Health Care Practitioners and past President of the Canadian Federation of Aromatherapists.

Jan teaches in Canada, Netherlands and the UK, and offers various diploma courses in: Cosmetic Making, Aromatherapy, Reflexology and Aroma Cosmetology - Holistic Skin Care.

Jan also tutors at the Shirley Price College, UK and New Directions Aromatics, Canada. As well as being an author and a consultant, Jan regularly gives press, TV and radio interviews, and contributes to journals and magazines.